Relevant Programs that bring RESULTS!

www.MakeAWayNow.com

Keep It Moving

www.hustleuniversity.org

ISBN # 978-0-9825976-4-4

Published by: Hustle U Inc.

Manufactured in the United States of America

Printed by Selfpublishing.com

First Printing, March 2011

Photography by OPP Studios

PUBLISHER'S NOTE: This work is a labor of love. It is the result of my attending the School of Hard Knocks where I received a B.A. in *Failed Ideas*, a Masters Degree in *Bad Investments*, and a PhD in *Poor Time Management*. Names, characters, places, and incidents are either the product of the author's experiences or are used with permission, and any resemblance to actual persons, living or dead, business establishments, events, or locales is entirely on purpose. Resemblance to actual persons, living or dead, business establishments, events, or locales is entirely on purpose.

KEEP IT
MOVIN'

The World's #1 Strategies for Becoming
IMMOVABLE & UNSTOPPABLE

HUSTLE U INC.
New York   Atlanta   Los Angeles

TABLE OF CONTENTS

FOREWORD

I wrote this book for many reasons; but all of these reasons can be traced back to one emotion…. **frustration**.

Yes, my friends, I get frustrated too. The difference between me and most people though, is that my frustration leads to another book. Other people's frustration leads to anger or misery. One is destructive; the other is debilitating, both are non-productive.

And this brings me back to my point.

I'm frustrated with people's inability to see that the only thing holding them back in life is **themselves**.

Why can't they just *keep it movin'*?

I spent years providing free counseling, coaching and mentorship to people from all walks of life. They would each be able to make small, quick improvements in areas of their personal and professional lives; but within a month's time, most of them would eventually hit a wall. This wall would totally derail them from their path.

But this isn't what frustrated me.

What really bothered me was how they would try to rationalize their responses. After seeking my advice and following my instructions for weeks, all of the sudden, they didn't want it anymore. They felt as if they knew what was best for them. Their responses were *emotional*, so they didn't care anymore about my *logical* conclusions. Their responses were due to False Evidence Appearing Real (FEAR), so they ignored the *truths* that we agreed upon earlier. They turned stupid, because although they knew better, they weren't willing to DO better; and it is said that even God himself is helpless against stupidity.

So I became frustrated.

Greek mythology tells tales about the gods blessing individuals with the gift of prophecy, and then later cursing them so that no one would ever believe them.

Was this me?

I had the solution to a mysterious problem, the cure to a deadly disease. I had the answer to millions of people's problems......but they wouldn't *listen*.

Maybe, they will **read**.

So here I go again!

- Hotep

ABOUT THE TITLE

While the cover may display one of many variations, the actual title of this book is **"How to Become an Immovable Object and an Unstoppable Force"**.

As a fan of Marvel comic books throughout the 1980's, one of my favorite characters was a super-villain named, *The Juggernaut*. I was first introduced to him in a Spiderman issue. I even remember reading the tagline that said, *"Nothing can stop The Juggernaut"*. He was a huge muscular guy that wore a bronze, metallic suit of armor with a large dome-like helmet.

(Sounds kinda corny now).

Anyway, The Juggernaut's power was derived from this armored suit and helmet, which when intact, made him superhumanly strong. The suit also created an impenetrable force of energy around his body. He became known as an unstoppable force because with this super strength and energy shield around his body, nothing could stop him once he began moving.

In one comic, they pit Juggernaut against another massive character and posed what I later learned was an age-old physics question: *What happens when an unstoppable force meets an immovable object?* This is where I first recall hearing these 2 phrases.

Twenty years later, the phrase was resurrected in my mind a little differently. During a conversation with my cousin, I found myself trying to motivate him to move forward with his plans to pursue a career in professional golfing. He was questioning his ability and making excuses for why he wasn't ready for golf. I told him he needed to be like *the Juggernaut* because I knew that name would make him recall the same

9

images of the character knocking down buildings and throwing everything in his path to the side that I remembered too.

It worked!

My cousin immediately understood what I was saying to him. He stopped making wimpy excuses and started to man up and refocus his mind on achieving his goal. For some reason though, I mistakenly thought *the Juggernaut* was the immovable object AND the unstoppable force. So I told my cousin to write this down as a reminder:

I am an Immovable Object
and an Unstoppable force.

And thus, a mantra and the title of this book was born.

INTRODUCTION

Feel like you've been dealt a bad hand?
Wish there was more time in a day?
Tired of slow progress?
Working hard, but have nothing to show for it?
Sick of "going through it"?
Wondering how some people make success look so easy?
Always feel like your project isn't quite ready?
Something bad always happens right before you are ready to make a big move?
Find yourself "stuck" in life?
Lost a loved one?
Seem like you just can't get ahead?
Feel like you are going in circles?
Suffering from a broken heart?
Are people hating on you?
Have you lost it all?
Are you too giving/ nice?
Is it hard to tell people "No"?
Feel like nobody wants to help you?
Too many people owe you money?
Don't know where to start?

If you are reading this book, then you are standing at the starting line. And when you've finished, I will have shown you how to overcome any adversity you encounter and go from trials and tribulations to triumph.

If you want to change your life, you first have to be willing to change yourSELF. Not **who** you are, but *how* you are.

Within these pages, I will demonstrate that our current situations are not as much due to the events that happen to us, but are more due to how we **deal** with these events. In other words, people's lives aren't bad because they **have** problems; their lives are such because they don't know how to effectively SOLVE problems.

BE WARNED!

Some of what I write will make you laugh, but other parts may make you upset or cause you to remember negative past experiences. This is ok. There is no gain without pain. Allow this book to provide therapy and healing to those wounds. Read it as many times as needed. Keep it with you in your book bag, pocket book; download it to your computer, laptop or tablet so you can access it daily.

Life is a system of problems and solutions! So read on, as I provide an extensive assortment of solutions to life's most common problems, the keys to becoming IMMOVABLE and UNSTOPPABLE!

WHAT IT MEANS TO BE IMMOVABLE AND UNSTOPPABLE

The Immovable Object:

An immovable object simply cannot be moved. A person becomes immovable when he/she is able to use the power of resolve to create an impenetrable field of energy around themselves. This "force field" enables them to block out all would-be distractions and interference that life has to offer. No insult, no coaxing, no pressure, no person, no emotion, no incident, no headline story, no catastrophe can move this person from their center. They will hold their position.

The resolve of a person who becomes an immovable object is admirable. History books and documentaries tell stories of the lives of men and women who would not be moved. There are hundreds of famous quotes that speak to the nobility of being immovable. However, a person that is an immovable object can also be very dangerous...especially to THEMSELVES.

To be immovable, one has to have made a conscious and permanent decision about something. Their resolve forms the "force field" which will allow nothing to change their mind in regards to this decision. Unfortunately, many people are poor decision makers. Others make uninformed decisions. When bad, uninformed decisions are made by people who are immovable, they become dangerous.

Mistaking their ignorance and stubbornness for strength and heart, many people are immovable to a fault. Some are foolish enough to stand resolved on a position that has been proven wrong, just to show how immovable they are. This person, although immovable, will be destroyed. They will be broken into pieces like a statue by the forces of truth and justice.

However, when a person is on the right side of truth, is wise, patient, clear-thinking and a problem solver, they can use the techniques in this book to empower their lives as an immovable object.

Reverend Dr. Martin Luther King Jr. is the epitome of the Immovable Object. As the most recognized figure in the African-American Civil Rights Movement, he is revered, respected and honored world-wide for his ability to stay unmoved and on course in the face of some of the most horrible conditions.

Dr. King set out to accomplish his goal (racial equality in the eyes of the law) by using non-violent means. His path was beset by violence at every step. His home was bombed. People made verbal threats against him and his family. He was physically assaulted at peaceful marches. He received daily threats in the mail. He was stabbed; and his friends were attacked (and some even killed).

Throughout all of this mayhem, Dr. King remained unmoved and stayed his course of non-violence. By doing so, he was able to achieve his goal. In appreciation of his efforts, we celebrate a national holiday in his honor and most major American cities have a street named after him.

Imagine the impact YOUR EFFORTS can have on the world once you become an **Immovable Object**.

The Unstoppable Force:

An unstoppable force cannot be stopped. A person becomes unstoppable when he/she is able to use shear will power to create a great field of energy around themselves. This "force field" enables them to pass through all the trials and tribulations that life has to offer. No mistake, no failure, no injury, no loss, no person, no institution, no handicap, no disease, no economic downturn, no war, no government, no condition, no natural disaster can stop this person. They will forge ahead.

There will be roadblocks that can slow the unstoppable force down. However, if they are observant and wise, overtime this person will develop other characteristics and habits that will improve their speed. These habits will help this person build the type of lifestyle that will reduce the frequency and size of the roadblocks.

A person can be an unstoppable force, but without wisdom, they will find themselves moving at a snail's pace through life because they haven't learned how to reduce the frequency and size of the roadblocks they will face. They become drunk with power and find so much enjoyment in overcoming roadblocks, they actually create more trials for themselves just to prove they can't be stopped.

The wisdom in this book will not only help you become unstoppable; it will also assist in making roadblocks light as a feather and others will simply disappear!

Sean "Diddy" Combs is a great example of an Unstoppable Force. He set his sights on becoming a successful record industry executive. Along his journey there were many roadblocks and tragedies. Someone was killed at a concert he produced. He got fired from a prestigious record label. He almost went to jail for gun and bribery charges. His famous girlfriend (a woman he loved very much) broke up with him. Critics said he wasn't a good rapper and dismissed his music production. His good friend and top-selling artist (the Notorious B.I.G.) was murdered. But Diddy always proclaimed in his songs that he *"can't stop and won't stop."*

And he didn't.

Despite all of the troubles and tragedies, Sean Combs has persevered. Today he owns **Bad Boy** Record Company, a chain of restaurants called **Justin's**, a clothing company named **SeanJohn** and a number of other businesses. He has reality TV shows of his own and also executive produces shows for MTV, BET and VH1. To this day, in the face of all the critics, he still releases his own albums featuring himself as an artist. Like the man said…he can't stop.

Imagine the things YOU can accomplish once you become an **Unstoppable Force**.

HOW TO BECOME
IMMOVABLE
AND UNSTOPPABLE

1. Know Your Goals

The first key to becoming immovable and unstoppable is deciding on a clear goal. Without knowing your goal and having the vision of its attainment firmly fixed in your mind, you will be easily distracted. All the great empowerment books and programs agree on this point.

By knowing your goal and staying focused on it you can literally will yourself to accomplish it. You can train your mind to "scan" for opportunities. You can convince other people to believe in you. You can block, circumvent or hurdle over many of life's common troubles.

A person that doesn't know their goals is like a navigator with no destination. They are just sailing aimlessly in the ocean. Their boat will go anywhere the tide takes them.

Like the saying goes, *"Stand for something or you will fall for anything."*

If you don't have goals you will become a victim to the will and agenda of others. You will end up bouncing aimlessly from relationship to relationship, job to job and circumstance to circumstance. Because of YOUR inability to set or stay focused on YOUR goals, you will have little or nothing to show for your life.

The Bottom Line: Before setting out to become immovable and unstoppable you must first know your goal(s). The rest of this book will help you stay focused on them.

2. Start With (and Keep) the End in Mind

The shortest distance between two points is a straight line. However, most of our life journeys are not straight paths; they are more like zig-zags. The more zig-zags we make, the longer it will take for us to reach our goals. Here is one way to reduce the amount of zig-zags that occur in our paths to success.

Start With and Keep the End in Mind.

Along your journey, you will be faced with an incredible amount of choices. Having so many options can be overwhelming. At times, you may have difficulty deciding which choice to make. If you know your goal and keep it in mind, this will make the decision-making process easier. It will also lead you to make BETTER decisions.

This is how it works. When you have a number of options to choose from, all you have to do is decide which choices will bring you closer to your goal. Then eliminate all the options that will take you away from your goal. From there, choose from the options left over. The more clearly fine tuned your goal is, the easier it becomes to make the best decision every time!

The Bottom Line: Start your journey with the desired result (goal) in mind. Keep this goal in mind as much as possible. By doing so, it will help you make better decisions when faced with multiple choices so you can *keep it movin'*!

3. Focus on Solutions

Life is a system of problems and solutions. Why are most people overwhelmed by the problems? Because that is where they focus most of their attention! When you ask how they are doing, they have a checklist of problems to share with you. They complain about their problems, write about their problems. Some try to drink or smoke their problems away (which usually creates more problems).

Try instead, focusing your attention on the SOLUTIONS to your problems. Brainstorm solutions. Discuss the solutions. Write the solutions down. The more you focus on solutions, the more your brain will seek out solutions and make you more aware of the solutions that are all around you. Some you will find are right under your nose!

The Bottom Line: Everybody has problems; they are a part of life. Switch your focus from the problem to finding the solutions and you will soon be asking yourself....*Problem? What problem?*

4. Make Haters your Motivators

People hate on others because they feel threatened by or envy them. The only reason why you would have haters is because you are excelling at an activity. Your haters either think you are getting attention and rewards that they should get, or they wish they could do what you do. This means that haters come with success. They are a byproduct of it.

You need to decide (right here and now) whether or not you want to be successful. If so, then you must also accept that people will envy your accomplishments. Some will cheer you on; others will try to tear you down.

The key to dealing with haters is not to engage them. Do not argue with or instigate haters. This is a waste of time and diverts your focus in the wrong direction (which is exactly what they want). Simply recognize the haters exist and *keep it movin'!*

Remember, if haters are starting to appear, this is an indication that you are doing well. The better you do, the more they attack. So, haters can be used as gauge for your success. Haters are a good thing to have; love your haters! Their appearance should motivate you to keep going. Turn their negative hate as positive fuel for your engine and *keep it movin'!*

The Bottom Line: Haters are an unfortunate byproduct of success. If you are (or want to be) successful, you will have haters. Ignore them for they are pitiful people. Convert the energy they are using to BREAK you, into part of the energy that MAKES you!

5. If the Shoe Doesn't Fit, Don't Wear It

Name-calling and insulting others is something that mature people stopped in elementary school. Unfortunately, most people haven't matured past that point. (For example, many adults can't read beyond a 5th grade level.) It's no wonder that we see such buffoonery on reality TV. The fights, incessant yelling, meaningless arguments and silly drama are all indications that many people need to go back to pre-school.

It's bad enough when they're in your face. It becomes worse when they spread rumors or letters. Now, with blogs and other social media, these idiots are free to spew hate and insults across the World Wide Web.

What can you do to stop it? Nothing! You can't stop people from doing or saying what they want. You CAN fight them or try to insult them back, but this only causes more retaliation. On top of that, it diverts your attention from your real goals.

Although you can't stop the insults, you CAN deal with them in certain ways so they aren't as hurtful or distracting. One of these ways is by not allowing untrue comments to faze you. *If the shoe doesn't fit, don't wear it.*

This means, if a statement is made about you that isn't true, don't entertain it. Don't give the person who said it or the energy of their words any value or respect by turning it into a big deal. More often than not, by doing this, the statement fades away into obscurity and the person who said it looks like a fool for even making such an absurd comment.

The Bottom Line: We give power to ideas and people that we entertain or engage. Yes, we should attempt to make sure false or incorrect information is not spread about us. But if we find that this mis-information is the result of someone trying to cause trouble….ignore it; and ignore them. They are probably just another hater attempting to take you off your hustle. Why are they so concerned about you anyway? *Keep it movin'!*

6. Don't Take it Personal

Sometimes people will attack you by bringing up embarrassing, personal or negative things about you that actually ARE true. What can you do to stop it? Again, nothing! But here's another strategy that will help you deal with these buffoons. *Don't take it personal.*

The truth is, people are selfish. They are always thinking of themselves, their needs, wants, desires and especially their feelings. When people feel good, they normally DO good things. They smile, compliment others, help people and give of themselves. However, when people feel bad, they behave in the opposite manner.

There will be times when people attack you for no apparent reason. You will have experiences when strangers treat you in a foul manner without cause. When this happens….. *Don't take it personal.* They are not angry with you. They are not even thinking about you. They are having a bad day and you just happen to be the person in front of them. So don't take the attack personally. Brush your shoulders off and *keep it movin'.* You've got things to do!

The Bottom Line: People are selfish and care mainly about satisfying their own needs. When their needs are met, they treat others well. When their needs are not met, they treat others poorly. If someone treats you poorly, it's more a reflection on who **they** are, not you. So don't take their behavior/ actions personally. They've got issues. *Keep it movin'!*

7. Control your Emotions

When people allow emotion to guide their actions it often leads them to make poor decisions. The reason why this occurs is because emotions are an automatic response to stimuli. Emotions don't think; they FEEL. In addition, emotions have no gauge, so if they are left unchecked, they can wreak havoc.

The way to check our emotions is by using logic. Logic is the police that maintains control over our emotions. Without logic we act out of control. Some people (when they come to their senses, blame their emotions for their insane actions. This is totally UNACCEPTABLE!

The ability to use logic is what separates us from other mammals. If you are older than 6 years of age, you should be able to control your emotions. There is no excuse. Even if you believe that women are more emotional than men, there is still <u>no excuse</u> for an adult to allow their emotions to run wild and cause them to behave irrationally.

Anyone who cannot control his or her emotions is in need of serious intervention. Their life will be wreaked with drama, unnecessary struggles and legal problems. None of which can benefit the person who wants to *keep it movin'*.

The Bottom Line: Don't become a victim or prisoner of your emotions. Honor your emotions. Express how you feel. But don't let your emotions dictate your actions. THINK! Your emotions DO NOT excuse your behavior!

8. Stop Trying to Guess People's Reasons, Motives or Intent

Unless you are an officer of the law, please stop trying to guess people's reasons, motives or intent. Nobody owes you an explanation. If they won't freely tell you why they did something, you need to *keep it movin'*.

All too often we try to play detective in order to figure out why someone we care about did something that hurt us (ex-lovers, estranged parents, friends). We scratch our heads, ask around, meditate and pray. Some even go as far as seeing a psychic for answers.

It is true that knowing *why* things happen is important to understanding and improving our knowledge of the world. However, we can't force people to tell us what we want to know. Interrogation tactics don't help and often lead to forcing a person to lie.

Trying to guess a person's reason, motive or intent is a waste of time. Unless they tell you, you'll never know; and even if they DO tell you, there's no guarantee that they've told you the truth. So why ask why?

People have their own reasons for doing things. Sometimes their reasons are logical and make sense; other times their reasons are unbelievable and stupid. So what? What do their reasons have to do with you? Nothing; it's THEIR reason! Move on!

The Bottom Line: Stop playing detective! People have their own reasons, motives and intent for doing things. You are not entitled to, or owed an explanation for anyone's actions. If they won't tell you …too bad! If they DO tell, you can choose to accept their answer or reject it. The real truth is, **They did it because they wanted to!** Instead of wondering why another person did what they did, you need to be focused on what YOU are going to do. *Keep it movin'!*

9. Stop Chasing the Past / Bury the Dead

All of us have had negative experiences in our past. But if we are not careful, a negative past can hinder our present situations and permanently damage our future.

Some people have a habit of constantly bringing up negative occurrences from their past. If you are one of these people, please STOP IT! It's counter-productive behavior! Most of the time, bad experiences only serve to make us upset or angry. Replaying these experiences over and over is like self-inflicting pain upon oneself. Why would you do this?

It is normal for us to think about events and people that hurt us, but for some people, the thoughts grow into an obsession. This is when pondering a negative past becomes counter-productive and dangerous.

Wallowing in sadness due to a loss is counter-productive. Trying to guess why someone did you wrong is counter-productive. Getting angry and seeking revenge by retaliating against someone that did you wrong is counter-productive (and will probably lead to more trouble).

None of these responses lead to anything good; and each distracts us from our goals and can prevent us from achieving them.

There comes a point when a person's obsession with the past prevents them from moving forward. Be careful of this happening to you.

If you find yourself thinking so much about the past that it interferes with your present duties and prevents you from achieving your goals...... stop it! You can't afford to let this happen. You have a destiny to fulfill and nothing can get in your way.

The Bottom Line: You can't move forward into your future, if you are constantly looking back at your past. Get over it, and *keep it movin'*!

10. Stay Away From Troublemakers

Unfortunately, as certain as we are that there are good people in the world, there also exist bad people as well.

Some of you reading this have a hard time labeling people as "bad". You'd rather call them, *"good people behaving poorly"* or something like that. Likewise, some of you don't like making judgments about people. You believe that only God can judge whether a person is good or bad.

Well I'm here to tell you.....*you better wake up and smell the coffee!*

You NEED to start making judgments about people! Otherwise, you will be plagued by problems that other people will bring into your life!

Loud mouths, drug/ alcohol abusers, pranksters, liars, violent gang members, name callers, criminals and gossipers are all troublemakers. Stay away from them. I don't care if they are friends or family members. Find new ones!

Avoid troublemakers like the plague. If you see them coming in your direction...move. If they call you...don't answer. If you frequent the same area...find a new place to hang out. Troublemakers are always looking for suckers to recruit and join them in their mischief making. They enjoy making trouble because they themselves suffer from misery and problems (and misery loves company). Don't become their next victim.

If you don't join them, some troublemakers will try to play on your ego by calling you scared, lame or trying to guilt or dare you into their world of foolishness. Don't fall for it! It's not a matter of you being scared; it's a matter of you being SMART! You've got business to handle, things to do, people to see and money to make. You don't have time for the drama.

*In the rare instances, there will be troublemakers that target a certain individual and consistently try to cause trouble for them. This is called a **bully** (also known as a stalker, bug-a-boo, scrub, loser and buster). Bullies are miserable people with no lives of their own, so they become fixed on others. If you are the victim of any type of bullying and you've already asked the person to leave you alone, please consult the local authorities. Don't try to confront a bully; by doing so, you will play right into their hands. Let the professionals handle the problem and keep it movin'.*

The Bottom Line: There are people in the world who are up to no good. They are constantly in trouble themselves or making trouble for others. Don't allow them to pull you into their world of madness. Stay away from these people, lest their troubles become yours. If you need to, let the proper authorities remove an insistent troublemaker from your life. Taking these matters into your own hands should be your last alternative. Why? Because you're so busy *keepin' it movin'!*

11. Don't Let People's Issues Become Your Problems

(Some of you might disagree with this one. That's probably because you need this advice the most!)

People have issues. Some of their issues are their own fault, others aren't. But their issues are certainly not YOUR FAULT!

Most of us are kind people who want to help others in need. I believe each of us does so in our own way. However, there are also a large percentage of people who are giving to a fault. That means, they give things that they don't have, or they give so much, it begins to take away from their ability to meet their own needs. This is a **problem**.

Another problem is when we allow people's issues to spill over our lives as we try to help.

This is what I call, *"letting other peoples issues become our problems"*. And if you are someone that allows this to happen...STOP IT IMMEDIATELY!

Learn to draw the line. Learn to say *"No"*. If you don't, you will unnecessarily subject yourself to a world of trouble; trouble that isn't even yours to begin with.

Helping and giving to others in need is one of the greatest joys we can experience. Don't spoil this joy by giving so much that it becomes **painful**. Here's a guide to help you decide WHEN and HOW much to give of yourself.

1) Give as long as what you have left is enough to meet your needs and short-term goals.

2) Help as long as your assistance does not expose you to physical harm, legal sanctions, and financial hardship.

* You may also want to consider the potential emotional and psychological damage getting involved can cause you.

I know it sounds mean and selfish, but just because someone else is *"going through it"* doesn't mean you have to as well. Their issue is not your problem. Do what you can (if anything at all) and *keep it movin'*!

The Bottom Line: Everybody has issues. Issues are a part of life. It is good to help people overcome their issues (just like you would hope someone would help you overcome yours). But, if there comes a point when helping a person with their issues becomes a problem for you, you need to draw the line and stop helping. Don't let people's *issues*, become your **problem**!

12. Stop Gossiping

Gossiping is a big waste of time. It is an activity for people who don't have anything worthwhile going on in their own lives, so they concern themselves with the lives of others.

The unfortunate truth is: most gossipers actually DO have something more worthwhile and important to do, but they are NOT doing it because they are too busy gossiping!

Gossiping includes talking about the lives of peers, co-workers and celebrities; but it doesn't end there.

Most men don't consider themselves to be gossipers. They may even chastise women for gossiping about their girlfriends and neighbors. But some of these same men are actually HUGE gossipers themselves. They gossip about their favorite professional teams and athletes!

Many men spend a considerable amount of time gossiping about the lives of athletes. *Who is the best player? Who has highest stats? Who makes the most money? Who is getting traded? Who said what about someone else?* They even have TV and radio shows purely dedicated to nothing but sports gossip!

GET A LIFE!

Stop gossiping and find something more constructive to do with your time. Use it to engage in an activity to bring you closer to your goals. Create something, make some money, exercise, plan, write, build, spend time re-connecting with family and friends.

The Bottom Line: You've got enough going on in your life. Why be so concerned with the happenings in someone else's? Stop gossiping! Don't worry about what other people are doing; focus on what YOU'VE got to do! *Keep it movin'!*

13. Turn Pain Into Power

There is one way to use negative experiences as a source of strength. Painful experiences from our past can be used as a place of power.

Negative experiences hurt us and cause pain. Most of us respond to this pain with sadness or anger. For many, the sadness and anger can be debilitating and stifle progress.

However, pain can also be used constructively. To do this, a person must first identify negative experiences as a natural and necessary part of life. When these "bad" experiences occur, they have to seek the lesson that can be learned from it. Then, they can use the experience as a source of power.

Use mistakes from the past as lessons to prevent similar mistakes in the future. Use painful experiences as motivation to strengthen/ empower yourself so they won't be as painful if they happen again.

You can use your overcoming of negative experiences to teach others how to do the same. Share your story in a book. Maybe someone will want to make a movie about your incredible story of triumph! But remember, first you have to overcome the experience and prevail. So *keep it movin*!

The Bottom Line: Don't let past failures, losses or pain stop you. Use them as sparks of ignition for your engine and take action!

14. Live Beneath Your Means

The U.S. is a country of excess. Many of us have become accustomed to a lifestyle filled with things we don't need. Our natural desires for life, liberty and happiness have been tainted by the pursuit of riches and fame, which has led to greed and immoral behavior.

Corporate led media has hypnotized Americans. Through their onslaught of commercials, endorsements and other marketing schemes, they have most of us believing we need the newest and fastest gadgets, the biggest and most luxurious homes, the most recent cars, the perfect bodies and at least a million dollars, all right now!

The pursuit of perfection and riches has caused widespread insanity amongst many Americans.

For the attainment of mostly unnecessary and superficial symbols of success, many are willing to sacrifice their own life, and the lives of others! Some resort to stealing, lying, cheating, enslaving thru debt, prostituting themselves and even killing.

The sad thing is that we've been sold an image of success and happiness that is based on material gain and not on how we actually feel. Each of us has our own measure of success, and it takes different things to make us happy. Stop letting corporations define success and happiness for you. Their job is to keep you feeling unhappy and unsuccessful so you will continue buying their products.

The result of this massive consumerism is people living far above their means.

Wise people know that being rich is not about how much money you make, but more about how much money you KEEP! Therefore, they learn how to live beneath their means.

Some people think they "going through it" because bad things are happening to them. This is often NOT TRUE. The reason why they got stopped in their tracks is because they couldn't defend themselves when life "happened".

Bad things happen to everyone. They are a part of life and can't be prevented. However, through proper decision-making, we can reduce the amount of bad things that happen to us and minimize their impact by defending ourselves.

One way we build a strong immune system against the negative events in life is by living beneath our means.

People who live above their means are setting themselves up for major trouble. Their high-risk behavior exposes their vital life functions to outside forces and leaves them unprotected. When life "happens", they will have no means to protect themselves because their finances have already been overextended.

Most people think that living AT their means is a good idea. While living this way is definitely better than living above ones means, it still poses a problem. Life doesn't always "happen" one event at a time. Sometimes, we can suffer multiple bad events consecutively. A person that lives at their means will be able to defend themselves from one event, but after that, their defenses will have been spent. They will be unable to suffer another attack, and we all know the saying, "when it rains it pours".

The best way to defend yourself from the bad events that occur in life is by living <u>beneath your means</u>.

Adjust your lifestyle so that you are able to save money every month. Save some of it, invest some of it too. Decide on an amount to save that you feel will adequately help you defend yourself from 2-3 life events (usually 2-3 months pay). After you've accumulated that amount, you can decide to keep saving or maybe even invest the additional amount to make your money work for you.

This is how you prepare yourself for when life "happens", so you don't have to *go through it* like other people.

The Bottom Line: Live beneath your means so you can *keep it movin'* even during times (like a recession) when most people's progress has been slowed down or stopped altogether.

15. Don't Catch Analysis Paralysis

This is a very common problem especially amongst creative people. It also causes problems in people's romantic relationships as well. Be wary of Analysis Paralysis (AP).

Analysis Paralysis occurs when a person over analyzes a plan, creation or opportunity to the point that it is never sufficient. In other words, a person who suffers from AP needs perfection before they will move forward; and since perfection is seldom ever achieved, this person rarely moves forward.

Sometimes people justify their lack of action by saying things like, "I'm still planning for the project," or "I'm waiting for the right time," or "I'm not quite ready." It is true that planning, timing and preparedness are elements for success. However, for people who suffer from AP, nothing is ever good enough, the time is never right and they are never ready. Their over-analysis is combined with a pessimism that creates a habit of non-achievement.

Don't let yourself become stricken with Analysis Paralysis. Don't try to justify your lack of action by thinking you just have "high standards" or are some sort of "perfectionist." (Don't kid yourself). Success requires ACTION! Ask any successful person and they will admit that they often didn't always have the best plan, nor did they always feel prepared or ready for an opportunity…they just DID IT.

Like them, your fortune will be realized by continuously moving forward in the direction of your goals. By moving forward (even when you don't think you are at your best), you will begin to build the muscles, learn the lessons, develop the resources and meet the people you will need to build, and more importantly, maintain your success.

The Bottom Line: Planning, quality and timing are all very important elements for the success of an idea; but don't let the lack of perfection hold you back from taking action. Sometimes, you have to just do it! The truth is that PRACTICE MAKES PERFECT. So keep it movin' forward towards your own perfection!

16. Use What You Got to Get What You Want

This phrase was once made popular by women who used their bodies to get money or material items from men. Although it is still relevant in the previous context, this phrase can be applied in a much broader sense and become even more empowering.

First, we can use it to recognize that we all have natural talents and skill sets that we can use to reach our goals. This is, after all, what the happiest people in the world do. They get paid doing what they either love to do, or do best. In essence, they are *using what they got, to get what they want.*

Secondly, we can use the phrase to remind us to start with what we have, and where we are, to move forward even though we don't have the best of conditions. As stated in the previous chapter, life seldom provides perfection. We create perfection through refinement. In order to refine something, it must first start out as rough and imperfect. Then we apply a refining agent to smooth it out.

YOU are a work in progress. YOU are rough and imperfect. Your action (moving forward) is the refining agent that creates the friction that smoothes your conditions into better, more perfect ones. So don't worry if what you have isn't the best. If it is all you have, then use it! Use what you got, to get what you want!

The Bottom Line: Instead of trying to figure out what you WANT to be or do, start with recognizing who you already are or what you already have. I guarantee you

will be able to *keep it movin'* even when you thought
you had nothing left.

17. Get Over Your Fear of Failure

Much of people's lack of action comes from a fear of
failure. Nobody likes to fail. It's disappointing, and (at
times) embarrassing. Unfortunately, failure is a
necessary part of life.

If you can accept this fact, then why fear failure? Why
fear something that is guaranteed to happen? Instead,
we should find ways to embrace it. And since we know
it will occur, we should also prepare for it.

Embrace failure because it is helpful. Failure helps us
because it lets us see where we need to improve.
There is a lesson to be learned from every failure. If
you are able find the lessons hidden in your failures,
you will learn to embrace and appreciate your failures
as opportunities for improvement.

People who are able to prepare for failure are best
positioned to keep it movin'. When failure occurs, the
prepared person can: Troubleshoot, solve problems,
remain cool-calm-collected, get up, brush their
shoulders off, and keep moving forward. Without
preparation, a person responds with: surprise, panic,
stress, drama and halting of progress.

The Bottom Line: There are times when you will fail;
but failure doesn't have to define your life.

Remember popular statements like:

No pain, no gain!

Without struggle, there is no progress.

Embrace failure. Prepare for failure. Learn from failure and use this new knowledge to *keep it movin'!*

18. Stop Complaining...
DO Something!

People love to complain about what they feel is wrong in the world.

Complaining is a big waste of time; first, because nobody cares about YOUR problems. They have enough of their own.

Secondly, because most complainers are also part of the very same problem they are complaining about. Why? Because they aren't DOING anything to solve the problem!

Most successful people view complainers as annoying whiners (losers) who contribute nothing to the world, yet expect it to be perfect.

The only people who enjoy the company of complainers are other complainers. They get together and have a big "pity party" to voice their complaints, gossip, critique and defame others. All of this is counter-productive and destructive behavior.

It is ok to voice your opinion about something you believe is wrong, but if you are going to do so, please also be working on a SOLUTION to the problem! Share your solutions with others. Build a team! Work on the problem together.

The Bottom Line: If all you do is complain about a problem, then you are PART of the problem. Don't talk about it, BE about it!

(To those who complain, but don't want to help solve the problem: please shut up and *keep it movin'*!)

19. Don't Fret About Things you Can't Change

In life there are 2 types of events that occur: those we can change, and events we can't change.

One major reason why some people get stopped in life is due to the fact that they spend too much time and energy trying to change things that can't be changed.

Here are things that can't be changed. Any attempt to change these things is futile.

- The past
- Other people
- Nature's laws

The past has already occurred. It is done! Focus on your future.

You can't change another person. People can only change themselves (and even that rarely occurs). So stop trying.

Nature's laws have been around since the beginning of time. They do not change and will not until the end of time. Learn the laws. Accept the laws as a necessary part of life. Don't attempt to fight or cheat natural law. You will lose!

The Bottom Line: There are things in life we can change, and others that we cannot. Accept this fact! Once you do, you can let go the burden of trying to effect things that you have no power over. Then, you can pour all your great energy into the things that you CAN impact and keep it movin'!

20. Persistence Overcomes Resistance

"Keep throwing darts; you will eventually hit a bullseye." -Hotep

"Persistence is just like having faith, because if you didn't have faith, you would not persist." -Earl Nightingale

Life is filled with resistant forces. Trials and tribulations are all around us and more are guaranteed to come. The only way we can triumph over trials is through forward motion. We have to "go through" the trial. If we don't, it will always remain.

Some trials are more resistant than others. For example, one trial may be easy to pass through as if walking through a thin sheet of rice paper. Another trial may be more like trying to walk through a mountain made of solid stone. Only one force can wear down a solid stone mountain......... persistence.

Persistence is the same force that allows drops of water to erode through solid rock and metal.

You must become like water. Year after year, drop-by-drop you must persist towards your goal. If you do, you will find all resistance "erodes" away; even the most resistant forces on earth.

Persistence and resistance go hand-in-hand. In order to strengthen our body's muscles, we use resistance to force them to work harder and grow stronger. The same goes for ability to persist.

We need resistance to force us to persist. The stronger the resistance, the more it makes us work, therefore, strengthening our endurance and power to persist. This is how we become unstoppable.

The Bottom Line: The only force that can overcome resistance is PERSISTANCE. Success may not come as quickly as you want it, but if you *keep it movin'*, it will come. Life yields to the person who is persistent!

21. Stop Making Excuses, Make it Happen!

No one wants to hear excuses for failure. Most people don't believe the excuses they hear anyway. Even if the excuse explains a valid reason, the end result is still the same...FAILURE.

Here's a secret way to reduce the need to make excuses...*make it happen*!

When a person makes excuses, they begin to believe they can't do a certain thing. Once that happens their brain begins to stop working on the problem. It no longer considers success as an option because it is convinced that the certain thing simply can't be done.

However, when a person is intent on "making it happen", their minds shifts from thinking it CAN'T be done, to brainstorming ways it CAN be done.

This is a major difference between successful and unsuccessful people.

If you adopt the habit of "making it happen", you will find yourself accomplishing more things in less time and with less effort.

The Bottom Line: Where there's a *will*, there's a *way*. Instead of explaining all the reasons why you CAN'T do something, think of all the ways you CAN do it.

22. If you Can't Join 'em..... Beat 'em!

Of course this is a play on the old expression: "If you can't beat them, join them."

I've always had a problem with this expression because it insinuates that we should first strive to compete with or conquer others and if we can't, then we should just give up and be a part of their team as a sign of defeat.

I disagree.

I happen to believe that we should first strive to cooperate with others. If they don't want to work with us, then we should show them what they missed out on by becoming successful without them (maybe even in spite of them)!

There are times in each of our lives when we want to be a part of something, but for some reason...can't (like a group, club, job etc.)

I say: "If you can't *join* them...**beat** them."

Instead of begging to be down with a group that doesn't want or appreciate you, start your own!

If you get fired from a job, start your own business! If you get kicked out of a group, start your own organization! Then, use your pain from the rejection as fuel to make your business or organization even bigger and better than the one that dismissed you.

DID YOU KNOW that after being fired from Disney, John Lasseter founded **Pixar Animation Studios**? John's work was so amazing that Disney later had to come back to him to hire his company (of course this time, they had to pay much more for his services). This is how the classic animated movies; "**Toy Story**" and "**A Bug's Life**" were birthed. John Lasseter couldn't join Disney, so he beat them!

The Bottom Line: Success is the sweetest revenge. You don't have to attack or belittle anyone to "beat" them. If a person or group won't accept you, *keep it movin'*. Build your own empire without them. Make it great; make it shine! Your brightness will cast a shadow on anyone who didn't accept you in the past.

23. Let It Go

Pain, betrayal, anger, loss, abandonment, mourning, sadness, envy, embarrassment and rejection are natural responses to hurtful events in our lives. It is OK to allow ourselves to experience these feelings in order to heal. However, these same feelings will become toxic and poison our minds, bodies and spirits if we don't learn to let them go.

Holding a grudge (or negative emotion) is non-productive and potentially hazardous to our health.

It's not productive because it keeps us focused on the past and people/events that have hurt us. Instead, we should turn our attention to the future and people/events that will be good for us.

Negative emotions are part of our natural healing process, but they will become hazardous if we don't let them go. When unchecked, negative emotions begin to harbor (make a home) within us. These emotions become hungry and they only feed off of other negative feelings. They begin to "eat" at us. Then, like a virus, they begin to multiply. This is how experiencing negative emotions turns from being part of the healing process, to becoming cancerous, long-term depression.

Let these emotions go for your own sake and sanity!

The Bottom Line: Allow yourself to feel negative emotions/ responses to hurtful events. Recognize HOW and WHY you feel the way you do. Give yourself some time to process your feelings and reflect. After that, put it behind you and *keep it movin'!* Let it go, cuz life goes on!

* I recommend giving yourself 7 days to accept, feel, process and reflect on a hurtful event. In my opinion, anything beyond 10 days means a person is beginning to wallow in self-pity and submerging themselves in negativity.

24. Forgive…but Never Forget!

Along with letting negative emotions go. We must all learn how to **forgive**.

When people feel guilty for doing us wrong, they often seek forgiveness. Since we are upset with them, we tend to refuse their request as a way to "strike back at them". This is a HUGE mistake!

Forgiving helps avoid the hazardous effects of pain. Forgiveness is how we let pain go so it doesn't consume us. Therefore, forgiving is something that we must do for our **own** benefit, not for the other person!

The truth is: people often seek forgiveness not for its own sake, but as a way to restore their relationship with another person back to what it once was. HERE IS WHERE YOU "STRIKE BACK"!

Calmly let them know that you DO *forgive* them, but you won't *forget* what they did. Therefore, you won't be dealing with them anymore. You are moving on!

The Bottom Line: When people do you wrong, forgive them. Forgive because it's in YOUR best interest to do so. But never **forget** what they did. Learn the lesson from the experience so it doesn't happen again. **Remember** the pain it caused you and use that memory to power your drive to *keep it movin'*!

25. Stop Playing the Blame Game

"BLAME is what people do when they don't want to take responsibility for their own lives." – Hotep

When we blame another person, what we are inadvertently saying is that the other person is in control of the situation. (They are in charge, that's why it is "their fault".)

I don't know about you, but **I'M THE BOSS OF ME**!

As long as you blame others for the events in your life, you will always have to wait for others to **change** the events in your life. You will always be a victim. You will always be at the mercy of other people's will. You will be nothing more than a puppet!

Stop blaming other people for what happens in YOUR life. It's YOUR life, not theirs. Step up and take ownership of yourself. When things go well, the credit is yours. When things don't go right, the fault is YOURS too!

The Bottom Line: YOU are the captain of your ship. If you blame others for what happens to your ship, then you have obviously given control to someone else. Take back the controls of your life and accept full responsibility for what happens in it. If you don't like the direction it is headed in, change it. If you DO like the direction your life is headed, then *keep it movin'*.

26. Change Your Environment

There are different types of environments: places where we live, work, play, visit or hang out. All environments are NOT equal. Some are made up of rich, fertile soil; others are wastelands. Some environments have lots of precipitation; others are like deserts.

Organisms have been known to be able to survive in some of the harshest conditions; but if you can, don't subject yourself to such environments. MOVE to areas that best support your goals.

We have a tendency to become like the places we live in. This is due to our natural ability to adapt to our environment. People who live in areas that are plagued with poverty, violence, crime and ignorance tend to become like then environment in order to survive. Likewise, people who live in healthy, positive and affluent areas become like their environment as well. This explains why the rich get richer, and the poor get poorer.

We become like where we are from.

It's not impossible to succeed in life when a person comes from harsh living conditions, but it is more difficult. So, if you recognize that you are in an area that is beset by any form of negativity, please make it one of your goals to change your environment.

If you **live** in one of these harsh environments, try to move. If you can't move, find nice places to visit or hang-out.

If you **work** in a harsh environment, try to get a new job. If you can't find one, make one. If you can't make one, decide on a hobby that can take you to places where you can "get away".

The Bottom Line: We adapt to our environment. Therefore, improve your chances for success by living, working, playing, visiting or hanging out in environments that are conducive to affluence, growth, peace, happiness and freedom.

27. Roll with the Punches

When life "throws its blows", instead of constantly trying to block or meet them with force, try rolling with the punches.

Rolling with a punch is a fighting expression. It means to go with the flow of the attack in order to avoid its impact. A fighter does this by turning his/her body in the direction of the blow, thereby sidestepping the attack and forcing the opponent to waste his/her energy by missing. After a while, the opponent will have expended so much energy trying to hit the fighter, he/she will become tired. Then the fighter can easily mount an offensive attack of his/her own and win the battle.

You too can roll with the "punches" that life throws at you. When people attack, sidestep their blows and let that negative energy pass right by you. Let your opponents waste their time and energy trying to attack you by making them miss. Meanwhile, you are calm, your energy is reserved and you stick to your plan.

Blocking blows and counter-attacking are common responses to attacks. They are not "bad" responses; they simply lead us away from the goals we have set for ourselves. By blocking people's attacks you end up absorbing the energy of their blow. Then you have to get rid of all that negative energy you allowed them to transfer to you. By constantly counter-attacking, you allow your opponent to set the pace of the battle. Then you will end up fighting THEIR fight instead of devising your own game plan.

The Bottom Line: Most people's attacks are not worth the time and energy it takes to reply. Try first to roll with the punches. This will allow you to avoid harm, as well as help you save your strength for the important things (like *keeping it movin'*)!

28. Choose the Right Partner

Two heads are definitely better than one, but only if you choose the right partner.

In my third book, **The Hustler's Gospel**, I go into detail about the *Value of People* as being one of the 7 values of wealth and power. The true value of people is due to what I call the "Multiplier Effect". People multiply the areas in which they are proficient.

This means if a person is intelligent, by partnering with them you will multiply intelligence in your life. However, the "Multiplier Effect" works with both positive and negative attributes. That means if you partner with a person who is depressed, it will multiply depression in your life. So choose wisely.

Let me be clear that by partner, I not only mean business partner, but also (and more importantly) your life partner or mate.

In his classic book, **Think and Grow Rich**, Napoleon Hill explains that *Wrong Selection of Mate* is the most common cause of life's failure and brings about misery, unhappiness and lack of ambition.

The Bottom Line: People bring both their positive and negative traits into any partnership. Your most important partner is your mate. If you choose wisely, your partner will be a great asset to your life and multiply your speed and power (and therefore your ability to *keep it movin'*). If you choose poorly, you are setting yourself up for serious problems.

29. Learn How to Cut People Off

You are on a mission. Along your way, you will meet people who interfere with your progress. They are known as **Time Wasters** or **Time Takers**. Some will interfere on purpose; they are easy to identify because they are offensive. However, others will waste/ take up our time by accident. These people are often a little more difficult to handle.

Examples of people accidentally getting in your way are those that want to talk to you about their issues, vent, gossip or discuss things that don't really matter or concern you. They might want something from you. They may be interested in you (but you are not in them). They won't let you off the phone. They interrupt you while you are trying to work. They take longer than their allotted time slot. These are the people who come in the way of your progress, but don't really mean to.

When good people inadvertently interfere with our progress it's difficult to manage. We know they don't mean to be in the way, but yet...they are.

What can we do?

Most of us have a habit of allowing ourselves to be subjected to accidental time wasters/ takers because we don't want to be rude. But as a goal-driven people on a mission, we don't have time to waste. We must learn how to politely cut people off.

Cutting people off doesn't have to be rude. In fact, if you are proactive about the situation, you can avoid being offensive. When a time waster/ taker starts talking your ear off, you probably become restless. You may even begin to tune them out. Eventually you will become impatient with them. If you don't address the situation before this point, you might get so fed up with the other person that you say something mean out of frustration.

Before it gets to that point, try cutting them off. Cut people off in a humble yet firm manner. Use phrases like, *"Excuse me"* or *"I'm sorry"* but don't do it in a weak manner or they will not take your attempt serious. Try not to make them feel like it's their fault. Limit your interactions with them. Don't make promises to call them back. Instead, use words like *"Maybe"* or *"Possibly"*. Hopefully, they will get the hint.

For those that don't, tell them that you are busy. Let them know that you are trying to accomplish some things and you can't speak right now. If you must, don't answer or return their calls, texts or emails. (Anyone that persists after this point is a stalker! You might need to call the police and report them.)

The Bottom Line: Don't let people waste/ take up your time. Their wants and needs are not any more important than yours; so don't feel bad if you have to cut them off. Be polite when attempting to cut people off, but do so in a firm manner. Don't make the other person feel like it is their fault. If they still get offended…too bad. You've tried your best to be nice about the situation, your conscience is clear, so *keep it movin'.*

* Note: Of course, it is a good thing to be there for someone in need, but some people are simply too needy, too talkative or complain too much. Whatever you do, just make sure you don't end up giving more of yourself to others than you give to yourself. You must prioritize and decide who is actually worthy of your time. As much as you would like to, you can't help everyone. See the section called, **"Don't Let People's Issues Become Your Problems."**

30. Don't Let Pride Get in the Way

Pride is an emotion that results when our ego is stimulated. When we make an accomplishment, we feel a sense of pride. We feel pride when someone pays us a compliment. However, pride can also impact us negatively if we do not keep it in check.

There will be times in each of our lives when our ego (self-image) is threatened or becomes under attack. Sometimes we have to do things that we may feel are "beneath" us. Some acts (or individuals) embarrass us. People may try to temp our ego by challenging or daring us to do certain things. Don't let them do it!

Don't let your pride get in the way of your success!

Keep your goals in mind. If you have to do embarrassing (but legal) things to accomplish your goals, do them! If you have to ask for help, ask for it! When people challenge, dare or otherwise try to "punk" you, don't fall for it! Don't allow them to manipulate you by using your pride as bait.

Keep your pride in check. A healthy ego is important to our success; but too much of anything is bad for us. Allow your feelings of pride to serve your needs to feel good about yourself, but be careful not to let others turn it against you.

Don't allow them to have such power over you. Stay strong, firm, on course and unmoved.

The Bottom Line: Don't let pride get in the way. Move it aside and *keep it movin'!*

31. Accept & Embrace Change

It has been said that the only thing in life that is constant, is change.

Change is guaranteed to happen. Although we may not always like the change, sometimes we are better off accepting it.

Everything that has a beginning will eventually come to an end. This is the natural cycle of life. People change. Opinions change. Plans change. Rules change. Feelings change. What can you do about it? Nothing.

If you think a certain change is going the wrong way, it IS possible to lead change in a different direction. However, that just means you've made an **alternative change**, you have not stopped change from occurring. Change will always find a way. Change must happen.

Instead of fighting change, learn to USE change to achieve your goals. Pay attention to upcoming trends. Position yourself to take advantage of these new developments. This is how successful people find the right time to make a move. This is how visionaries stay ahead of the curve. They see the change coming, accept it, embrace it and prepare for it.

The Bottom Line: Change happens. It can't be avoided. You can try to redirect change, but you cannot stop it. So accept it, embrace it and use it to your advantage and *keep it movin'.*

32. Avoid Unnecessary Arguments

Think about your last argument.

Was it necessary?

Think harder; think further back. Can you remember ANY argument that was necessary? Probably not.

A **disagreement** is when two or more people voice differing or opposing opinions about a particular topic. In a disagreement, each person thinks their opinion is valid and they share it with the other(s). What results is a discussion of the varied opinions to explore their validity. Sometimes the people simply recognize their opinions as being different and move on. (This is known as "agreeing to disagree.")

Disagreements are healthy because they allow us to explore different views, consider others' experiences and reflect on other opinions. In short, disagreements help us grow intellectually.

Unfortunately, some disagreements turn into arguments.

An **argument** is when two or more people attempt to force their differing opinions on each other. Most arguments are counter-productive because no one likes to be forced or bullied into anything. Arguments also tend to lose sight of the initial opinion that started it because the people involved often become emotional which leads to yelling or fighting. In the end, instead of changing people's minds, an argument often ends up hurting people's feelings (or worse).

If you start out trying to prove the validity of your opinion but instead, end up in a fight, you have FAILED to accomplish your goal. Arguing is counter-productive and unnecessary. Avoid arguments and argumentative people. They are both a waste of time.

The Bottom Line: Arguments are seldom (if ever) necessary. When engaging in a discussion, state your opinion. If someone disagrees, calmly discuss it to find out if you can see things from their perspective. If not, agree to disagree and *keep it movin'*!

33. Choose Your Battles Wisely

Although you might make all attempts to avoid all of life's roadblocks, pitfalls and detours, there will still be times when you have to fight.

Fighting should be a last resort. Not only because it often leads to more fighting, but also because fighting is a reactive response.

Many people get unnecessarily slowed down (or even stopped) from achieving their goals because they are tired from fighting too many battles. Battles are time consuming, energy draining and harmful to our minds, bodies and spirits. It is for this reason that it is of extreme importance to choose your battles wisely.

Most battles are simply distractions. They take us off of our paths by causing us to divert our attention to things that seem *urgent*, but are really not <u>important</u>. If not careful, people can find themselves spending more time fighting life than actually living life!

Many battles are simply NOT worth fighting.

One way you can determine if a battle is worth the effort is by determining what you stand to gain from winning the battle. Is the prize worth the effort? If not, then why fight?

Another way to decide which battles to fight is by being realistic about your chances of winning. If the probability is low, why fight?

A third way to answer this question is to decide whether or not winning the battle will bring you closer to your ultimate goals. You may end up winning the battle, but losing the WAR.

The Bottom Line: In each of our lives, there will come a time when we will have to fight for something; but these fights can be kept at a minimum if we choose our battles more wisely. Use wisdom and well thought out judgment before engaging in battle. Don't get caught in a cycle of fighting your way through every battle in life. You will find yourself worn out; without enough energy to *keep it movin'.*

34. Consider the Consequences

Although this book is all about moving forward, something must be said about pausing to consider the consequences of our decisions.

When driving a vehicle, at every turn, before every lane change, we have to take at least a brief moment to check the traffic conditions first. Likewise, before we proceed with our endeavors, we should also consider the consequences of our moves. If we don't, we are certain to cause many "accidents".

The Bottom Line: Every action has its reaction. Every cause has an effect. Before you make any move, always consider the positive and negative consequences. If the negative outweigh the positive, you may want to re-consider the move. If you are comfortable with the consequences, then *keep it movin'*.

35. Remember Where God Is

Not to get too religious, but it was once said that, *"The kingdom of God is within you."*

If you agree with this statement, then you should already know that you were born to be immovable and unstoppable. In fact, this power is in your DNA.

So remember where your creator is. Remember that his power lies within you. Use the strategies in this book to guide your innate power in the right direction.

The truth is, the only thing in the world that can move or stop you....is YOU!

The Bottom Line:

"People are often unreasonable, illogical, and self-centered; Forgive them anyway. If you are kind, people may accuse you of selfish, ulterior motives; Be kind anyway. If you are successful you will win some false friends and true enemies; succeed anyway. If you are honest and frank, people may cheat you; Be honest and frank anyway. What you spend years building,

someone could destroy overnight; Build anyway. If you find serenity and happiness, they may be jealous; be happy anyway. The good you do today, people will often forget tomorrow; Do good anyway. Give the world the best you have, and it may never be enough; Give the world the best you've got anyway. You see, in the final analysis, it is between you and God; it was never between you and them anyway."

-Mother Theresa

ABOUT THE AUTHOR:

Hotep is president and founder of HustleUniversity.Org, the first self-help HBCU for entrepreneurs. He is an internationally renowned success strategist, Congressional Award-winning educator and entrepreneur known for his out-the-box thinking, guerilla marketing tactics, branding expertise and his unique "no nonsense" approach to teaching leadership, entrepreneurship and practical business best practices.

Hotep's work has earned him nominations as a CNN Hero and for the U.S Presidential Citizen's Award. Hotep calls himself a "Business Abolitionist" and considers entrepreneurship as the key to freedom for all people. He is also the author of several popular empowerment books including the phenomenal classic; The Hustler's 10 Commandments.

Hotep says, *"With the right mentality there is nothing that can STOP you; with the wrong mentality, nothing can SAVE you!"*

To Book Hotep for Speaking Contact:
404-294-7165
hustleuinc@gmail.com
www.HustleUniversity.Org

OTHER PROGRAMS:

Intervention Guide, Workbook, DVD, Texbook & Poster

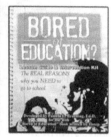

Poster, Lesson Guide/ Intervention Kit & Textbook

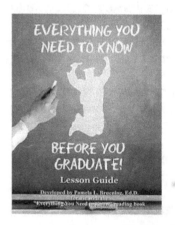

Lesson Guide & Textbook

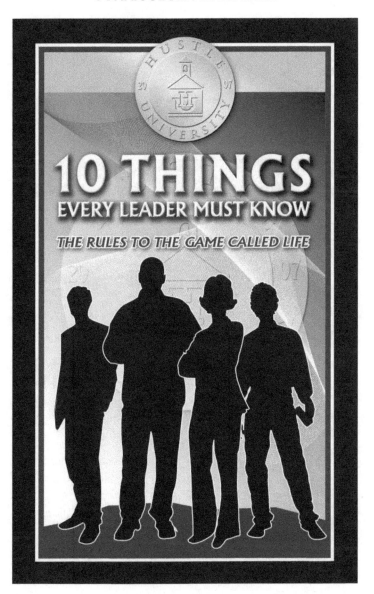